OLD OMAN

Most early drawings of Muscat are inaccurate. This mid-19th century engraving, after a painting by W. P. Witherington, is an exception. It shows Muscat from the north – from beyond the Mukalla cove, looking across Fort Merani (on the right) to Jalali on its high rock. The old palace is depicted, beyond the prow of the three-masted boum. Inshore fishermen (foreground, right) are bringing in a catch, avoiding a wreck of which a spar sticks out above the water. Several other single-sail houris in the background are plying across the harbour.

Muscat — and Muttrah beyond — at mid-century

OLD
OMAN

—— W. D. PEYTON ——

STACEY
INTERNATIONAL

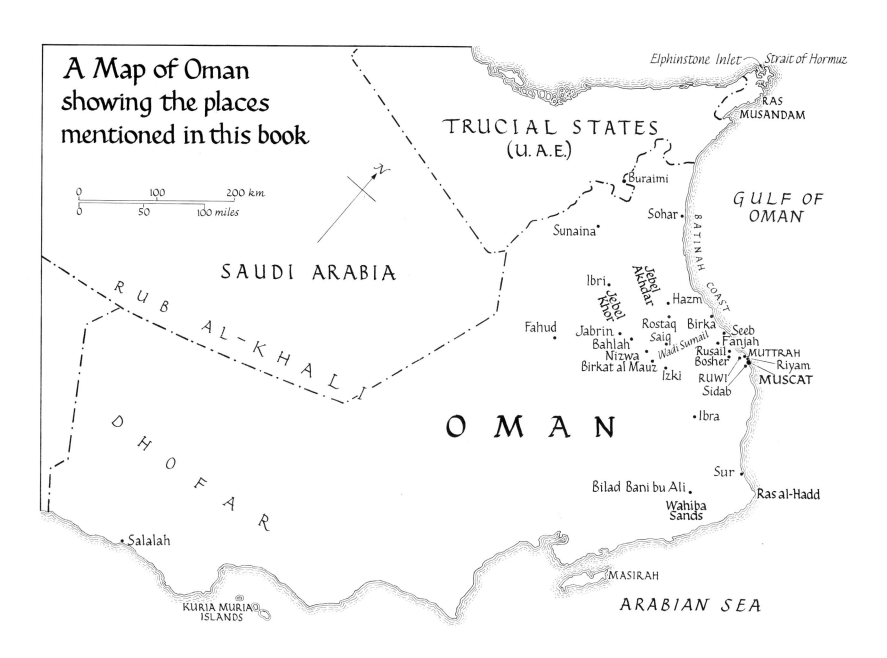

A Map of Oman
showing the places
mentioned in this book

Elphinstone Inlet — Strait of Hormuz

RAS
MUSANDAM

TRUCIAL STATES
(U.A.E.)

0   100   200 km
0   50   100 miles

Buraimi

GULF OF
OMAN

Sohar

BATINAH COAST

SAUDI ARABIA

Sunaina

Ibri
Jebel
Akhdar
Jebel
Khor

Hazm

Fahud

Rostaq   Birka   Seeb
Saiq   Fanjah
Jabrin   Wadi Sumail
Bahlah   Rusail   MUTTRAH
Nizwa   Bosher   Riyam
Birkat al Mauz   RUWI   MUSCAT
Izki   Sidab

RUB   AL-KHALI

OMAN

• Ibra

D
H
O
F
A
R

Sur

Bilad Bani bu Ali   Ras al-Hadd

Wahiba
Sands

• Salalah

MASIRAH

KURIA MURIA
ISLANDS

ARABIAN SEA

4

Author's Acknowledgements

We would first thank His Majesty Sultan Qaboos for his kindness in encouraging us to go ahead with the gathering and publication of photographs for the album. His Majesty's concern for the collection and preservation of the national heritage of Oman has been shown in many ways; among them the establishment of the Ministry of National Heritage and Culture, the collection of old documents and manuscripts, the setting up of museums at Qurm, in Bait Nadir at Muscat, and in the fort at Bait al-Falaj, the renovation of the palace fort at Jabrin, and the support and encouragement of the work of archaeological expeditions at Bosher, Sohar, Wadi Suq, Bat, Wadi Samad, Ras al-Junaiz, Ras al-Hamra, and other places.

His Highness Sayyid Faisal bin Ali Al Said, the Minister of National Heritage and Culture, has given us valuable help in obtaining photographs and with historical information.

Susan Larg and John Kimmins were responsible for the discovery of the Murphy collection. This collection, several albums and a number of loose photographs, was inherited by Pat Murphy of Burton-on-Trent from his father, Gerald Murphy, who was the Political Agent at Muscat from 1926 to 1930. Many of the Murphy photographs were taken by Mrs Murphy, now Mrs Charlotte Peirce of Eastbourne, Sussex, who went as a bride to Muscat on the appointment of her husband as Political Agent. We are most grateful to the Murphys for their trust in allowing us the use of a great many of their photographs. Some of the photographs in the Murphy collection appear to have been taken by Bertram Thomas.

Julian Lush, formerly of P.D.(O)., lent us his collection of photographs of the Ibri area in the early 1960s. Julian Paxton, of P.D.(O)., gave us our choice from the I.P.C. collection of 1951 photographs of the Muscat area. David Smiley's photographs of the Jebel War are a unique record as the official photographs of the campaign were lost.

In 1967, John Harris and Christopher Mitchell were the first to come to Muscat for the purpose of planning its development. We also thank Corin Purdon, Charles Cusick and others for sending photographs we could not use for various reasons.

W.D.P.

Editorial
Charlotte Breese
John Blackett-Ord
Sydney Francis

Design
Keith Savage

Cartography
Reginald Piggott

Old Oman
published by Stacey International
128 Kensington Church Street, London W8 4BH

© 1983 Stacey International
Reprinted 1989

ISBN 0 905743 34 2

Set in Linotron Baskerville by
SX Composing Limited, Essex, England
Printed and bound by
Lund Humphries, London, England

Acknowledgements
The publishers are grateful to the owners of the photographs included in this book for so kindly lending them. Page numbers and quantity of photographs, if more than one, follow the photographer's name.

Sayyid Abbas bin Faisal collection, 111; John R. Harris, 20-21, 21, 80, 112, 119, 121; John R. Harris & Christopher Mitchell, 116-117, 121; Paul W. Harrison M.D., 61; Captain G. Hewson, title page; Julian Lush, 79, 82, 83, 84 (2), 85, 86-87, 87; Ministry of National Heritage & Culture, Muscat, 45; Murphy collection, 22 (2), 22-23, 23 (2), 24 (3), 31, 32, 33 (2), 34 (3), 35, 46, 47 (2), 48 (2), 49, 51, 54, 55 (3), 56 (2), 57 (3), 58, 58-59, 59, 60 (2), 76, 77, 124, 125 (2), 126 (3), 127 (2); Thomas from Murphy collection, 62, 63 (2), 64 (2), 65 (2), 66 (2), 67 (2), 68 (2), 69 (2), 70, 71, 72 (2), 73 (2), 74 (2), 75 (4), 76; PD(O), 26, 27, 29, 30, 30-31, 39, 113, 114, 115, 120 (3); C. Pringle, 116, 122; Royal Geographical Society, 50, 50-51, 113, 124; Shell, 18, 20, 25, 28 (2), 80, 81, 88, 89, 90 (2), 91, 92, 93, 96-97, 97, 98, 100, 101, 102 (2), 103, 104, 117, 118, 121, 122, 123, 128; Colonel D. Smiley, 40 (2), 41 (2), 42, 105, 106, 107 (2), 108, 108-109, 109; Hank Snoek, 118-119; Private collection, 35, 36 (2), 37 (3), 38 (3), 38-39, 42, 43 (2), 49, 51, 61, 94, 95 (2), 96, 99 (2), 123.

Contents

Introduction

THIS album of photographs taken in Oman in the years from about the turn of the century to 1970 has two purposes. The first is to remind those Omanis and foreigners who were there during this period of some of the people and of the places where they lived, worked, travelled or fought. The second purpose is to show those Omanis and foreigners who were not there then what it was like in the not-so-far-gone old days.

Nearly three-quarters of the twentieth century passed before Muscat or Oman became reasonably well-known beyond the borders of the Sultanate. Even in such places as Cairo or Beirut a conversation might begin something like this:

'Where do you live now?'

'Muscat.'

'Moscow! What are you doing in Moscow?'

'Not Moscow. Muscat, in Oman.'

'Oh! Amman, in Jordan.'

'Not Amman – *Oman*, the southeastern corner of Arabia.'

In the early years of the century Oman had enjoyed a brief flurry of attention from European diplomats. From 1894, when the French government opened a consulate at Muscat, until 1913, when the last Anglo-French argument over rights and privileges was settled, serious diplomats and officials wasted a good deal of time and paper discussing what was whose in Oman. But, apart from a few Omani clients of either the British or the French, all of this had little to

do with how life was lived in Oman.

The ruler at Muscat was Sultan Faisal bin Turki who had succeeded his father, Sultan Turki bin Said, in 1888. By 1888, however, the great days of the Omani overseas empire were over. Except for Gwadur, a small enclave on the Makran coast which was sold to Pakistan in 1958, the empire was gone. The loss of Zanzibar and the prosperous East African possessions, in 1861, had weakened the basis of former Omani greatness. The opening of the Suez Canal, in 1869, reduced Omani maritime influence in the Indian Ocean. The increasing use of steamships made the once-powerful Omani sailing fleet obsolete.

Altogether, these disasters eroded the power of the Sultans in Muscat. In external affairs they became ever more dependent on the jealous protection of the British and the government of India. Internal affairs were even less orderly. The tribes of the Interior, though themselves rent in political twain as a result of the quarrels left over from the civil wars of the eighteenth century, staged rebellions in 1875, 1895, 1913 and 1915.

In October 1913, Sultan Faisal bin Turki died and was succeeded by his eldest son, Sayyid Taimur bin Faisal. By this time the fortunes of the Sultans had reached a low ebb indeed. The coastal area was raided by the Interior tribes for the last time in 1915 when a rebel force said to have numbered some 3000 was defeated by 700 Indian troops at Ruwi. A kind of peace was finally made between representatives of Sultan Taimur and the tribes of the Interior at a meeting at Seeb in September 1920. In later years it was suggested that the Seeb Agreement had been made between two sovereign states, but it was nothing of the kind.

From 1913 until 1954 the Interior was ruled by a succession of elected Imams whose relationships with the Sultans in Muscat were, apart from the occasional unpleasantness, reasonably amicable. Then, in 1954, a newly elected Imam,

encouraged by outside finance and intrigue, assumed the pretensions of sovereignty. His so-called State of Oman issued postage stamps – though there was no postal service; passports were issued – valid only in Egypt and Saudi Arabia; and an application was made for the State of Oman to join the Arab League. It was said that when the application was presented to the Arab League Council at Cairo there was an unseemly rush for a map to see where this unheard-of country might be.

In 1932, Sultan Taimur, who had always been a reluctant ruler, abdicated in favour of his eldest son, Sayyid Said bin Taimur, and went to live, first in Japan and then at Bombay where he died in 1965. Sultan Said inherited an empty treasury and a country that had few prospects of a bright future. This severe lack of money prevented his doing very much but he did establish the three Saidiyah schools, at Muscat, Muttrah, and Salalah. He set the finances in order, and sent six young Omanis off to Baghdad for further education.

What has become known as the 'Jebel War' took place in Oman on and off from 1955 to 1959. In December 1955, the Sultan took over the administration of the areas in central Oman formerly held by the Imam. The Imam, his dreams of independent statehood shattered, went into political retirement abroad. But he returned in 1957 for another round of revolt that enjoyed a brief success. In the end, however, with some British help, the Sultan's armed forces occupied the mountain strongholds at the end of January 1959, and the rebel leaders fled for the last time. The Sultanate was properly united again, for the first time since 1871, and Sultan Said bin Taimur ruled over all of it.

But the Sultanate was not to remain at peace. In Dhofar, where the local tribes had a long, almost annual, record of rebellion, trouble broke out once more. Its origins were obscure and probably trivial. Indeed, Sultan Said insisted that it all began when he sacked a gardener.

The Sultan tried to contain the Dhofari

rebels by using his locally recruited Dhofar Force but when, in 1966, some members of this group tried to assassinate him, he called in the Sultan's Armed Forces from Oman to take over the job.

The Sultan's Armed Forces had evolved over the years from 1921 when the Muscat Levy Corps was established at Bait al-Falaj. In 1953, the Muscat and Oman Field Force of four hundred men was set up to provide protection for oil exploration parties in the desert interior. In 1955, an administrative headquarters was set up at Bait al-Falaj, the regiments were designated in 1957, and in 1958 the establishment and expansion of the Sultan's Armed Forces as we know them today were made possible by a subsidy from the British government.

From 1965, the trouble in Dhofar grew into a more serious affair and attracted some attention in the international press. The Marxist success in the People's Democratic Republic of Yemen, and its support of the Dhofar rebels, left the western reaches of Dhofar open to highly subversive influences. A good deal of nonsense was written extolling the Marxist virtues seen in cooperatives, schools, and hospitals said to have been started in allegedly occupied parts of western Dhofar. In fact, these establishments, if they existed at all, were well over the border inside the PDRY but sympathetic foreign reporters had no way of knowing where they were taken.

The Omanis are the most even-tempered and tolerant among the peoples of Arabia. They were, however, given a bad name by early travellers who described them as fanatics when it came to questions of religion and dealing with foreigners. When the country was reunited after the Jebel War of the 1950s, the Sultan felt it wise to impose a touch of conservatism in order that the men of the Interior would not regard their fellow countrymen of the coastal areas as unduly frivolous or impious.

The complexities of business and social

life and the highly organised government bureaucracy found in Oman today did not exist before 1970. Business consisted mainly of the Omani and Indian traders and importers. Banking, from 1948 (when it began) to 1968, meant dealing with the local branch of the British Bank of the Middle East. Cable and Wireless ran the telephone system and handled overseas cables. Gray Mackenzie handled incoming shipments. Exports were limited to dates, dried limes and some firewood. Until 1961, the only post office was part of a British system in Eastern Arabia and the Gulf. The mission of the Reformed Church in America had a small general hospital at Muttrah, a smaller maternity hospital at Muscat, and a school, mainly for girls, also at Muscat.

The headquarters of the Sultan's Armed Forces was in the fort at Bait al-Falaj. The Defence Secretary, the Commander – who was seconded for two years from the British Army, and the Commander of the Sultan of Oman's Air Force had their families there,

but nobody else did. There were some seventy British officers of bachelor status, half seconded and half on contract to the Sultan. It was all fairly primitive: no plumbing in the fort or the barracks; the soldiers washed in the *falaj*; cooking was done on wood fires. After the Jebel War, units of the army were stationed, and lived in similar conditions, in the Interior at Seeb, Rostaq, Sohar, Sur, Izki, Nizwa, Ibri, and Buraimi. Any foreigner travelling in those parts was usually asked, 'Are you from the army or the company?' There were no other foreigners about.

The "company", Petroleum Development (Oman) Limited, was originally a member of the Iraq Petroleum Company group of companies but, from 1960, it was run by Shell which had 85 per cent of the shares. The other 15 per cent was held by the Gulbenkian interests. The other I.P.C. partners had decided, after failure to find oil at Fahud 1, that it was not worth carrying on exploration in Oman.

Oil exploration had begun with a base at

Duqm, on the Indian Ocean, but when the Interior of Oman became pacified after the Jebel War, a base was set up on the coast at Azaiba and a graded road built through the Sumail Gap. Azaiba remained the company headquarters until the new housing and industrial areas at Ras al-Hamra and Mina al-Fahal were built, in 1966.

Then it was possible for company employees to bring their families to Oman. Compared with anything else in Oman, the new company compound was a marvel of modernity. It had plenty of electricity, air-conditioning, a commissary with fresh food flown in from Beirut, a school with instruction in English and Dutch, and a well-equipped and staffed hospital. And there, by decree of the Sultan, the P.D.O. community lived behind guarded fences in isolation from the rest of the world. The Ruwi customs gate, near the present site of the al-Nahda hospital, provided a checkpoint for visitors to and from the oil company compound. Omanis who were suspected of carrying on with the foreigners (this meant no more than attending a movie or the occasional picnic on the beach) were reported to the Governor of the Capital by the gate keepers. The Governor then passed the information on to the Sultan at Salalah and he, in turn, ordered the Governor to warn offending Omanis that the Sultan disapproved.

Much has been said and written about the wretchedness of life in Muscat in the old days. There were, it is true, many restrictions and everyone was fairly poor. But there was, nevertheless, a feeling of community and everyone, Omani and foreigner, knew who he was and where he stood in that community. Everyone turned out for 'Id visiting, weddings, funerals, arrivals at Bait al-Falaj airfield, and speech day at the Saidiyah school. The managers of the bank, Cable and Wireless, Gray Mackenzie, and the oil company knew the families and problems of everyone who worked for them – and quite a lot about those who worked for the others as there

was considerable switching from company to company. Indeed, some of the more notable citizens of the Sultanate today began their careers in one of these companies, and worked for some others, before they were called into high government service. But opportunities were limited and some 75 per cent of those young Omanis who attended the Saidiyah school went abroad to seek work or further education, or both.

As for the government, well, the government was the Sultan. After 1958, the Sultan never returned to Muscat but there was a feeling that he kept an eye on everyone and on everything that happened there. He knew who everyone was and where they lived. He checked lists of employees of companies, requests to buy cars or boats, visa applications, bicycle licences (4 annas for six months), building permits (usually refused), and police and court records.

The Governor of the Capital, the Sultan's uncle, Sayyid Shihab bin Faisal, represented the Sultan on ceremonial occasions. The Minister of Interior, Sayyid Ahmad bin Ibrahim Al Qais, ran the day to day affairs of the rest of the country. The Wali of Muttrah, Ismail Rasasi, kept an eye on the Batinah walis and Sayyid Ahmad dealt directly with the Interior. The foreign advisers were always about. By 1970, there were Secretaries or Advisers for Defence, Finance, Development, Oil, and Courts as well as the Personal Adviser to the Sultan, Major Leslie Chauncy. On the whole, the country and the Sultan were well-served by these advisers who were ill-paid and restricted in their activities like everyone else.

The diplomatic corps was small. After 1947, the British Political Agency became a consulate and then a consulate general. There was also an Indian consulate general and that was all the resident diplomatic representation there was. Twice a year, on the Sultan's birthday and on the King's or – later – Queen's birthday, the government and the diplomats exchanged formal visits

as 21-gun salutes were fired from the eighteenth-century cannons at Fort Merani. Routine foreign affairs were conducted, always with reference to the Sultan, through the Personal Adviser by a single faithful and efficient Indian clerk in a gloomy room in an old Muscat house.

Among the more galling restrictions were those on travel inside the country. In general, Omanis from the coast were not allowed in the Interior and Omanis from the Interior were not allowed to travel to the coast, without permission. Foreigners were not allowed east of the British Consulate in Muscat or west of the oil company compound at Ras al-Hamra. There was some question where the Interior began for those purposes. Some held that the Interior began at the gates of Muscat, others, more generous, held that it began at Bait al-Falaj. Oil company employees whose work required them to travel were allowed to do so but their families were not. Mothers of children returning from school abroad to the company airstrip at Azaiba were graciously given passes signed by the Sultan so they could meet their children in the forbidden Interior.

The restrictions were, however, borne gracefully by both Omanis and foreigners. The communities were remarkably well-ordered and the rules were carefully obeyed. People did not travel to forbidden areas, women did not drive or wear short skirts, cars did not speed through Muscat, alcoholic drinks were not, openly, served to Omanis, lanterns were carried inside the Muscat walls when required, nobody smoked in public, or played music during Ramadhan. There was a good deal of grumbling by Omanis about the lack of business and educational opportunities and there were a few amateurish plots, mainly composed merely of wishful thinking, to get rid of the Sultan or get him to change his ways.

From the time, in 1964, when Petroleum Development (Oman) decided it had found enough oil to produce it profitably, a

number of people tried, with little success, to persuade Sultan Said to spend some money on the development of the country. The Sultan was, however, not only extremely cautious about spending money not yet actually in his treasury but also sincerely concerned about how modernisation and education would affect the people of Oman. He once said, 'The people shall not have what they want but what I think is good for them.' Nevertheless, by the time he was deposed in mid-1970, various projects were planned or begun. His only personal extravagance was the design and purchase of what he called an 'armoured yacht'. This ship, the *Al Said*, has since become the flagship of the Omani navy. But he never saw the ship because he made so many changes in the design that it was not delivered until after he was deposed. By the time he left Oman, having inherited a treasury that was more than empty in 1932, he had salted away some £100 million, nearly all in oil revenues, in twenty-four bank accounts. All of this was turned over to the new regime and was useful in the early development period.

Anyone trying to put together a photographic account of the period between 1900 and 1970 would naturally prefer an orderly progression of pictures of places, events, and personalities from the beginning to the end. But it does not work that way. People did not take photographs as casually as they do today and most of those that were taken are lost, faded, or just lying unknown and neglected in somebody's attic. An effort has been made to achieve a balance among the pictures of the various subjects covered. This has not been an easy task. A number of people have kindly lent us a large quantity of old photographs from their own collections or have made useful suggestions about where we might find others and we are most grateful to all of them.

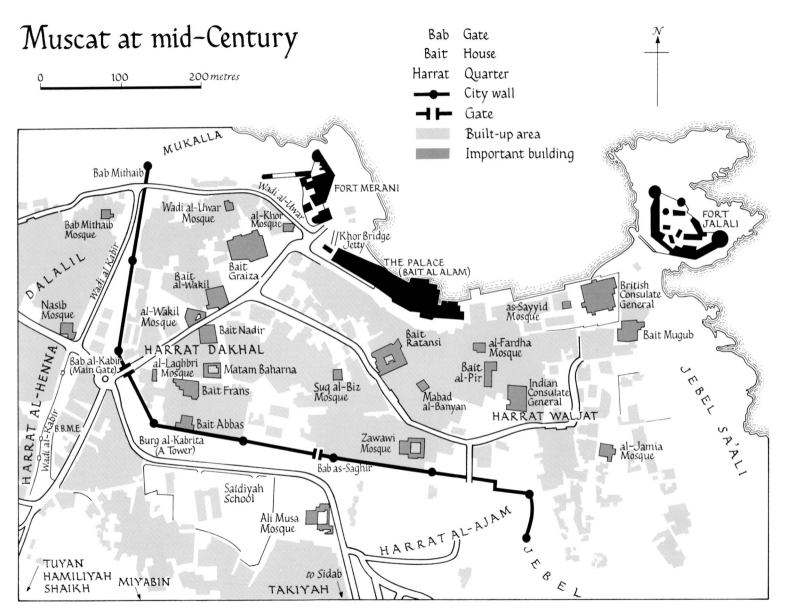

Muscat at mid-Century

0   100   200 *metres*

Bab   Gate
Bait   House
Harrat   Quarter
●━━● City wall
╼╀╾ Gate
Built-up area
Important building

N

MUKALLA

Bab Mithaib

Wadi al-Uwar

FORT MERANI

Wadi al-Uwar Mosque

al-Khor Mosque

Khor Bridge Jetty

Bab Mithaib Mosque

DALALIL

Wadi al-Kabir

Bait Graiza

Bait al-Wakil

THE PALACE (BAIT AL ALAM)

FORT JALALI

as-Sayyid Mosque

British Consulate General

Nasib Mosque

al-Wakil Mosque

Bait Nadir

Bait Mugub

HARRAT DAKHAL

Bait Ratansi

al-Fardha Mosque

Bab al-Kabir (Main Gate)

al-Laghbri Mosque

Matam Baharna

Suq al-Biz Mosque

Bait al-Pir

Indian Consulate General

HARRAT AL-HENNA

Wadi al-Kabir

B.B.M.E.

Bait Frans

Mabad al-Banyan

HARRAT WALJAT

JEBEL SA'ALI

Bait Abbas

Burg al-Kabrita (A Tower)

Zawawi Mosque

al-Jamia Mosque

Bab as-Saghir

Saidiyah School

Ali Musa Mosque

HARRAT AL-AJAM

JEBEL

TUYAN HAMILIYAH SHAIKH

MIYABIN

to Sidab

TAKIYAH

JEBEL

17

—— CHAPTER ONE ——

Muscat, Muttrah and Environs

THE population of Muscat began to dwindle from about 1856 when it was said to have been over fifty thousand. By 1970, it would have been hard to find five thousand people there. Nevertheless, the names of the old quarters (*harat*) were long remembered even when some of them had few residents. Inside the walls, the quarters, really neighbourhoods, were: Dakhal, inside the main gate; Waljat, east of the palace; Bab al-Mithaib, around the small gate in the wadi; and Wadi al-Uwar, from Bab al-Mithaib to the Khor jetty. Outside the walls, up the wadi from the main gate were Harat al-Henna, Tuyan, Hamaliyah, and Harat Shaikh. Outside the *suq* gate were Harat al-Ajam on the east, and Takiyah on the west up to the Sidab pass and, further west, Miyabin. Dalalil was between Harat al-Henna and

Muscat from the air, with a glimpse of Muttrah beyond, and Ras al-Hamra in the far distance. Beyond Fort Jalali (silhouetted against the sea) is seen the old coaling station. A 1960s photograph.

Bab al-Mithaib with Mudhabga nearby. The road to Sidab was opened for sturdy cars in 1961.

By land or sea, the approaches to Muscat and Muttrah delighted the eye of the weary traveller. They have continued to catch the eye of the photographer. The forts and the towers on the hills set the character of the two towns before one had actually set foot in them.

The dramatic panorama of Muscat as seen from the top of the pass on the road to Muttrah became everybody's favourite photograph. The entrance to Muscat has changed with the construction of the double carriageway through Kalbu but it is still possible to take the old road through Riyam.

The sea approach to Muttrah has changed with the addition of the corniche to the waterfront and, on the other side, the removal of the Arbaq tower and hills to make way for the new port.

Below *Muscat, mid 1960s, the old palace (demolished early 1970s) in the centre, and on its left the Diwan office a-building.*

Right *The official welcome to visiting vessels and notables was firing of cannon from Fort Merani's terrace by the Muscat garrison who lived in the Fort. The guns bear the arms of George III.*

Above *Muscat harbour in 1927, during the reign of Sultan Taimur bin Faisal, who was normally resident in Muscat.*

Right *Fort Merani, the Khor Mosque and part of Bait Graiza, in 1927.*

Above across the fold *An early 1920s photograph looks north across Dakhal. (Muttrah was reached from Muscat by sea.)*

Above and left *Fort Jalali – photographed in 1927 – built by the Portuguese in the sixteenth century. It was used as a prison. It is reached by stairs built up the rock face.*

Above *Two Indian mail ships are seen in Muscat harbour in 1926. All mail for the west from Oman was then routed through Bombay.*

Below *The tower in Wadi Kabir (1926) was supposedly built by the Portuguese to protect the water supply for Muscat – which in turn provided water to passing ships.*

Right *The water well. 1926*

Opposite *Muscat harbour from the customs jetty, in 1961.*

Right *Muscat's town and harbour, with the old coaling station in the cove of Mukalla, in the foreground, in 1961.*

Opposite Muscat is seen in a 1951 photograph from the top of the pass on the old road to Muttrah.

26

Below *A 1962 photograph shows the Dakhal quarter of Muscat, looking towards the eastern fortifications of the original wall.*

Right *This 1966 photograph looks towards the pass to Sidab, across the Takiyah and Harat al-Ajam quarters, with the Ali Musa Mosque centre left.*

Opposite *A view of Muscat in 1951, looking over the wadi, with the Laghbri Mosque in the foreground to the left and the house of Sayyid Ahmad bin Ibrahim, right.*

28

Above *Muttrah Fort in 1951. Beyond the bluff lies Muttrah town and harbour.* Right *In the middle distance, in the centre, is a small tower and an outcrop of rock which was to be flattened to build the new harbour. This ridge of rock once separated Muttrah from the former quarter of Arbaq, the ruins of which can be just discerned in the picture.*

Above *Muttrah customs house is seen in the 1930s, with a bundle of dates going out and firewood – also exported – in the background.*

CHAPTER TWO

The Ruling Family, 1912–70

THE rulers of Oman since 1741 have all come from the Al Said, or Al bu Said, family. They are descended from Ahmad Al bu Said, the Wali of Sohar who repulsed a Persian intervention and was elected Imam in 1741. The present Sultan, His Majesty Sultan Qaboos bin Said, is the thirteenth ruler from the family and eighth in direct descent from Ahmad Al bu Said. In 1900, the ruler was Sultan Faisal bin Turki. He was succeeded in 1913 by his eldest son, Sultan Taimur bin Faisal, who abdicated in favour of his eldest son, Sultan Said bin Taimur, in 1932. Sultan Said ruled

until July 1970. Members of the family were given the title of 'Sayyid'. Sultan Faisal had eleven sons. The youngest of these was Sayyid Abbas, a well-known figure in Muscat, who died in 1982.

Sultan Taimur had five sons and one daughter. Sayyid Said, the eldest, succeeded him; Sayyid Tarik became Prime Minister after July 1970 and died in London in 1980; Sayyid Fahar is Deputy Prime Minister for Defence; Sayyid Majid has held a number of positions, and Sayyid Shabib is a Minister of State.

Sultan Said had one son, Sayyid Qaboos, born at Salalah in 1942, and two daughters.

Preceding page *Three generations of the ruling family, c. 1912. Sultan Faisal bin Turki (seated) with Sayyid Taimur on his right and the infant Sayyid Said bin Taimur. Another kinsman is on the Sultan's left.*

Above, right *Sultan Taimur with his eldest son, Sayyid Said, c. 1915. Said bin Taimur became Sultan in 1930.*

Above, left *Sultan Taimur bin Faisal in the Al bu Said royal turban, and decorations.*

Above *Sultan Taimur on tour. He would often travel by camel.*

Right *Sultan Taimur bin Faisal.*

Further right *Said bin Taimur Sayyid with Bertram Thomas, then a member of the Council of State.*

Above *Sayyid Hamad bin Faisal, Wali of Sohar, the major town of the Batinah, in 1928.*
  Right *Sultan Said bin Taimur on the ramparts of Fort Merani – with Sultan Said's autograph.*

Above *Sultan Said bin Taimur dining at Salalah.*

Right *Sultan Said bin Taimur at the gate of Bait al-Alam, the Muscat Palace, in the mid-1930s.*

This page *Sultan Said bin Taimur.*

Above *Sultan Said bin Taimur with Sayyid Qaboos, his only son and heir apparent, at Salalah.*

Above, right *Sayyid Qaboos, now His Majesty Sultan Qaboos, at the Salalah Palace.*

Below, right *Sayyid Qaboos in England, 1963, after completing his course at Sandhurst.*

Left *Sayyid Qaboos in Mamura Gardens at
Salalah. 1966*
    Above *Sultan Qaboos visits Petroleum
Development (Oman) for the first time. August
1970*

Below *Sayyid Abbas bin Faisal with Brigadier Waterfield, Military Secretary, and Sayyid Thuwaini bin Shihab. About 1968*

Right *Sayyid Majid bin Taimur, Wali of Birka.*

Opposite, left *Sayyid Fahar bin Taimur with Melvin Watterson of PD(O).*

Opposite, right *Sayyid Sultan bin Hamad bin Faisal (left) with Hilal bin Badr, Court Poet. 1960s*

Below *Sayyid Ahmad bin Ibrahim Al Qais, then Minister of the Interior, with Sayyid Thuwaini bin Shihab in the 1960s.*

Right *Sayyid Ahmad bin Ibrahim Al Qais. 1960*

Below *Sayyid Tarik bin Taimur, right centre, receives 'Id callers. c. 1959*

Right *Sayyid Tarik bin Taimur at Muscat, 1970, when Prime Minister.*

—————— CHAPTER THREE ——————
The Society of Brotherhood, 1908

AT some time during the first decade of the twentieth century – it is believed that this photograph was taken in 1908 – the Society of Brotherhood was founded at Muscat. Sayyid Taimur, then heir-apparent, was the President. The purpose of the group was to present papers on literary subjects and to have poetry readings. It was not political or religious in orientation and its members included a number of the minority groups in the capital area. This photograph was taken in the Sidab garden of one of the members.

The most remarkable thing about the society was that it existed at all, in Muscat, in Arabia, in the first decade of this century. There were similar societies at the time only in Syria, Lebanon and Egypt.

From left to right, the members were: *Ahmed Darwish, Abdullah Katuri, Hamdan Mahmud, not known, Abd al-Qadir Zawawi, Sayyid Taimur, Abd al-Rahim Jafar, Saif bin Badr, not known, Zubair Ali, Muhammad bin Badr, Ali Sadiq.*

CHAPTER FOUR

Up the Batinah, 1927 and 1928

THE Batinah Coast begins at Qurm, not far from Muttrah, and runs uninterrupted for 175 miles in a generally western direction to Khor Fakkan and Diba where it meets the mountains of Musandam. It is the most densely populated area in the Sultanate.

It was the custom of Sultan Taimur to make an annual progress through the towns and villages of the Batinah, accompanied by a large entourage. There he held court, heard complaints and inspected local affairs.

The Batinah lived off vast date gardens and lime trees which also supplied the only exports. The dates went to India and the limes were dried and sent to Iraq and Persia where they were used to flavour tea.

Above *Sultan Taimur lands on the Batinah coast. 1928*

Right *Shaikh Ghusn bin Salim of the Bani Umr. 1928*

Far right *Shaikh Salim bin Diyan of the Bani Ka'ab. 1928*

Left *Sulaiman bin Madhafar, Wali of Khaburah. 1928*

Below *The fort at Khasab, at the head of the Musandam peninsula.*

Opposite, left *Sayyid Hamud, Wali of Suwaiq. 1928*

Opposite, right *Shaikh Ali bin Juma of the Bani Ka'ab. 1928*

Below *The telegraph station, on an island in Elphinstone Inlet, established a century ago.*

Left *The* Earl Canning *in Elphinstone Inlet, overlooking the Straits of Hormuz.*

Above *Sohar Fort – perhaps the oldest fort on the Batinah coast. In the twelfth century Sohar was one of the richest cities in the world, as an entrepôt of Farther Eastern trade.*

CHAPTER FIVE

The Council of State, 1928

THE Council of State was set up in 1920 as a four-man 'cabinet' to administer the state during the absence of Sultan Taimur in India and at Salalah. In 1928, the members of the Council were, from left to right: *Rashid bin 'Uzayyiz al-Khusaibi, for religious affairs; Sayyid Muhammad bin Ahmad, the Wali of Muttrah; Wazir Bertram Thomas, for financial affairs; and Shaikh Zubair Ali, for justice and the courts.*

CHAPTER SIX

Gwadur

THE enclave of Gwadur on the Makran coast was the last remnant of the Omani overseas empire. In 1871, Sayyid Turki bin Said had set sail from Gwadur to unseat Sayyid Azzan bin Qais as ruler of Oman. Gwadur continued to be one of the more neglected outposts of the Sultanate until 1958, when Sultan Said sold it to Pakistan of which it was naturally a part. Gwadur only had two claims to fame. It was a station on the Indo-European Telegraph, which was extended to Muscat in 1901, and it furnished Baluchi soldiers for the Omani armed forces.

Opposite *"Some of the lads of Gwadur"* –
*Gerald Murphy, Political Agent, third from the
left, and staff of the British Agency at Gwadur
(now part of Pakistan).*

Above, left *The British Political Agency.*

Left *High Street, Gwadur.*

Above *Imperial Airways* City of Delhi
*refuelling at Gwadur. (Imperial Airways was the
forerunner of BOAC).*

—————————— CHAPTER SEVEN ——————————

Opening the Muscat-Muttrah road
December, 1929

THE first road between Muscat and Muttrah was completed by the Muscat Levies under the command of Captain John Walker in 1929. The paving of the road was not, however, completed – to Bait al-Falaj – until 1961.

When the road was officially opened in December 1929, there were four cars to travel on it. They were: the chocolate brown Model A Ford Sedan which had come in November as a present to Sultan Taimur from the American philanthropist, Charles R Crane; the Delaunay Belleville belonging to Gerald Murphy, the Political Agent; a light lorry of unknown make that was the sole vehicle in the arsenal of the Muscat Levies; and the Morris of Dr MacKay, the Consulate Surgeon.

Preceding page *The Sultan and his party set out from Bait al-Alam, the Muscat palace. 1929*

Left *Mrs Murphy, the wife of the Political Agent, and Wazir Bertram Thomas await Sayyid Said bin Taimur.*

Above and below *The Muscat Levies are shown drawn up to await Sultan Taimur and the official party.*

Left *The grand opening of the road from Muscat to Muttrah. 1929*

Above *The arrival at Muttrah.*

—— CHAPTER EIGHT ——

Muscat main gate

UNTIL the road was built from Muscat to Muttrah, the western gate in the wall was usually called the Tuyan Gate, as it led to the wadi and the Tuyan quarter. There was little land traffic between the two towns. To get from Muscat to Bait al-Falaj, the sturdy traveller was rowed to Muttrah and there he mounted a camel for the rest of the journey.

After the road was built, in 1929, the gate became more important and in 1932 Sultan Said had it rebuilt. An inscription on a marble plaque was placed over the outside entrance saying 'Rebuilt by order of Sultan Said bin Taimur, Sultan of Muscat, Oman, Dhofar, and Gwadur, in the year 1354 AH'.

Above *A caravan enters Muscat, bringing provisions. c. 1924*

Far left *Muscat main gate from within the town.*

Left *Muscat main gate, seen from outside with part of wall and the Burg al-Kabrita tower.*

Right *Muscat main gate from the outside. 1951*

─────────── CHAPTER NINE ───────────

From Ras al-Hadd to Salalah, c. 1929

BERTRAM THOMAS was appointed Financial Adviser to Sultan Taimur in 1925 and was known locally as the 'Wazir'. He mixed his official duties with a love for exploration and spent much of his time travelling through the more remote parts of Oman. He achieved lasting fame when he crossed the Rub al-Khali from Salalah to Qatar in 1931, the first European to do so. He died at Cairo in 1948. The way to Dhofar from Muscat in 1928 appears to have been by dhow to Ras al-Hadd and then by camel and horse to the Bilad Bani bu Ali, through the Wahiba sands, and across the desert and mountains to Mirbat and Salalah.

Right *Ras al-Hadd, the most easterly point in Oman.*

Above *Sayyid Said bin Taimur visits Ras al-Hadd.*

Below *The fort at Bilad Bani bu Ali, sometimes in the past a troublesome tribal area, near the south coast.*

Far left *Amir Muhammad bin Nasir, Bani bu Ali.*

Left *Shaikh Bandar bin Nasir, Bani bu Ali.*

Right *On the battlefield of the 1809 engagement between a British landing force and the Bani bu Ali.*

Below, right *On trek in Wadi Ubaidhah, campsites were whenever possible found under trees.*

Above *In the Wahiba Sands, two women carry water pots to a well.*

Right *A well in Wadi Halfain, one of the great Oman watercourses.*

Above *A man and woman from the Mahra tribe by a frankincense tree.*

Left *Two Mahra collecting frankincense.*

Above *Shaikhs from the Qara tribe of Dhofar with staves. The man on the left is carrying a hand shield made of hardened leather.*
Right *Shakara tribesmen.*

Left *Shikait, a hill village with houses made of brushwood.*

Below, left *Cattle in the Dhofar mountains. Wealth in Dhofar was determined by the number of cattle owned by a family or individual.*

Left *Marbat*.
Right *Marbat Fort*.

Left *Taqa*

Below, left *Salalah, the al-Husn (palace) quarter.*

Right *A street scene at Salalah.*

Below, right *Al-Husn, the palace quarter, Salalah.*

Left *Sultan Taimur bin Faisal at Salalah.*

Above *An ancient stone monument of unknown purpose and origin, composed of trilyths.*

Right *The ruins of Balid, the mediaeval frankincense port.*

Left *Wazir Bertram Thomas on tour.*

Above *The Gate to al-Husn, the palace quarter.*

Right *Mamura Gardens, Dhofar. The Gardens are irrigated by their own* falaj *from the nearby mountains.*

CHAPTER TEN

I.P.C., Fahud, Ibri, Buraimi and the Interior, 1951–61

UNLIKE the other states and countries of eastern Arabia, Oman has had a settled population for hundreds, perhaps thousands, of years. Beyond the Hajar mountain ranges, in which the settlements nestled, lie vast desert areas where the bedouin lived, not in tents but under trees, and tended their flocks of goats and camels. While the great bedouin tribes of the north were deeply involved in the politics and the establishment of the modern states found there today, the bedouin tribes of Oman were not so involved. In general, however, they were left on their own and, of course, had their little wars and battles with each other, usually over territorial claims. When oil was found in Oman the oilfields were in bedouin territory.

This meant that the oil company had to deal with them, mainly for the hire of unskilled labour, in and about the oilfields. The company set up two bases for this purpose, one at Ibri to treat with the Duru tribe, in whose area all the earliest producing fields lay, and one at Izki. By the Sultan's order, both bases were close to army detachments. The bedouin shaikhs were a lovable but rascally lot who were meant to be, and were, kept in order by the Minister of Interior in Muscat. The company representatives at Ibri and Izki, who were Arabists of the post-imperial school, not only did their jobs for the company but they were friends, doctors, lawyers, electricians, plumbers and mechanics for the local communities.

Right *The camel market at Ibri, a busy place on market days.*

78

A well at Ibri oasis. The whirring noises from the wheels at the top could be heard from afar.

Above *In the suq at Ibri, mud columns hold up the split palm logs and barasti roofs.*

Right *Inside the Ibri suq, goods from the Trucial Coast are sold, as well as those from Oman.*

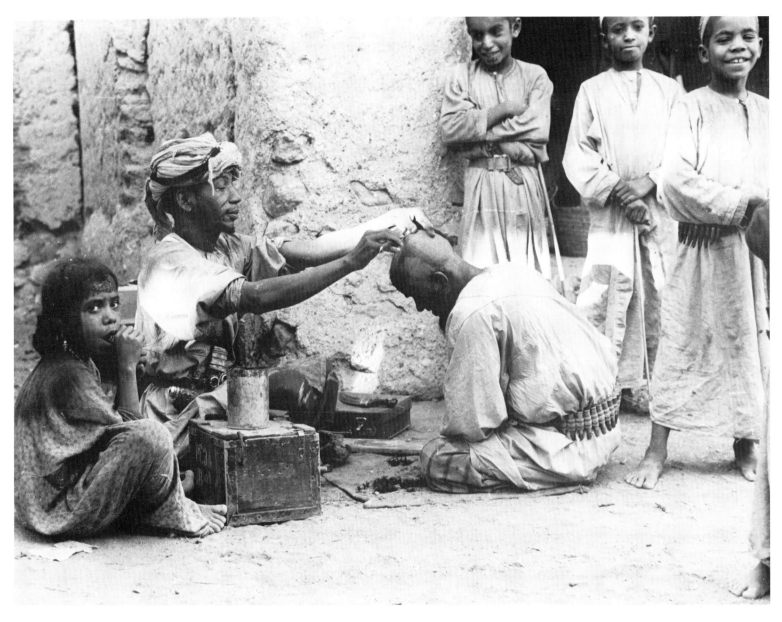

Left *The barber at Ibri suq attends a client from the desert.*

Right *A street at Ibri, including a typical unadorned* Ibadhi *mosque.*

Left *The village postman at Ibri. There was no official post but this chap collected the mail and saw that it went in the right direction. Remarkably, it usually did.*

Right *Sayyid Saud bin Harib, Wali of Ibri, visits the oilfields with the company general manager, Richard Clough.*

Above *The site of the first, unsuccessful, attempt to find oil at Fahud. This failure led some of the IPC partners to give up their interests in the Oman concession.*

The entrance to Buraimi Fort. 1962

Buraimi Fort, 1962. Three villages in the Buraimi oasis are in Oman territory.

CHAPTER ELEVEN

The Interior, Nizwa, Bahlah, Rostaq and forts

EACH of the towns of the Interior has its own character. Each has its own *falaj* system and each its supporting date gardens and market place.

Right *The town of Sumail in Wadi Sumail. Because of its rich plantations and abundant water, Sumail was fought over throughout Oman's long history.*

Far right *A* falaj *in a date garden. Wherever there is a village or a date garden it is watered by a* falaj *which brings the water from the mountains.*

Falaj *at Birkat al-Mauz.*

Above, Falaj *at Birkat al-Mauz.*
 Right *The great tower of the Yaruba at Nizwa. The Yaruba dynasty ruled Oman for about a hundred years until 1744.*

Above *Part of Nizwa, the capital of inner Oman.*
Right *Aerial view of Nizwa.*

Left *Colonel Hugh Boustead, the Development Secretary, addresses a gathering at Nizwa, 1959, during a fair held at the Government Agricultural Gardens.*

Right *Wind tower and fort, Bahlah, pre-1900.*

Below *Part of fort at Bahlah, before 1900. The fort is among the largest and oldest in the country.*

Above *The fort at Jabrin, before 1900. Jabrin was the fortified country seat of the Yaruba Imams.*
Right *General view of Rostaq, 1951. The Yaruba moved their capital to Rostaq better to oversee their coastal and foreign possessions.*

Above *A general view of Rostaq. 1951*

A young Omani at Rostaq. 1951

Sayyid Hamad bin Azzar's house at Rostaq, before 1900.

The fort at Rostaq. 1951

Right *The fort at Rostaq. 1951*
Far right *General view of the fort at al-Hazm, 1951. Al-Hazm lies midway between the coast and Rostaq.*

Far left *An Omani guide at al-Hazm. 1951*

Left *Washing hands after lunch at al-Hazm. 1951*

Right *Building a mud-brick wall at al-Hazm. 1951*

CHAPTER TWELVE
The Jebel War

THE Jebel War was a landmark in the history of Oman as it was the first event there of which real notice was taken in the world press. It also led to the reunification of the country and the establishment of the armed forces on reasonably modern lines.

Right *Wadi al-Hammah – the mountain terrain.*
Far right *David Smiley with the Al bu Shams Shaikhs at Sunaina, between Ibri and Buraimi.*

Below *Some of the Life Guards at rest.*

Right *Life Guards*

Above *Malcolm Dennison and wolf carcasses – strung up to warn their fellows not to raid the flocks – at Jebel Khor.*

Below and right *At Saiq, in the Jebel.*

Below *Sayyid Tarik bin Taimur and Colonel Deane-Drummond.*

109

CHAPTER THIRTEEN

Saidiyah School Speech Day, c. 1965

From left to right. *Hilal bin Badr, the Court Poet; Sayyid Turki bin Mahmud bin Muhammad bin Turki; Ismail Rasasi, Wali of Muttrah; Sayyid Ahmad bin Ibrahim Al Qais, Minister of Interior; Sayyid Shihab bin Faisal, Governor of the Capital; Major Leslie Chauncy, Personal Adviser to the Sultan; Sayyid Malik bin Faisal; Sayyid Sultan bin Hamad bin Faisal; Hilal Muhammad Said; K. B. Maqbul Hussein; Ramzi Mustafa and two teachers from the Saidiyah School.*

CHAPTER FOURTEEN
The Capital Area, c. 1970

THE area between Muscat, Sidab and Bustan on the east and Ruwi, Bosher, Ghala and Seeb on the west has, in recent years, been designated as the Capital Area. It is in this area that most of the residential, commercial and industrial development has taken place. It is hard to believe that so much has taken place so quickly. If, say, one had set out from Seeb for Muscat one would have seen only the few cabins that were then the P.D.(O) base camp at Azaiba, a few small houses at Hamriyah, the Bait al-Falaj fort and airstrip, and nothing else before the Muttrah wells.

The houri, *a dugout canoe, was the common taxi, fishing boat, and general means of transport before the coming of cars and the building of roads. A 1967 picture.*

Below *Setting out from Mukalla to receive cargo from a freighter in Muscat harbour. 1960*
Right *Muscat fishermen near the Khor jetty. 1951*

Left *Bundles of firewood were a minor export from Muscat. 1951*
Right *The Khor bridge, Muscat, 1951. In the background, the Khor Mosque and Bait Graiza.*

Below *Fort Merani and the Khor jetty at Muscat.*
1969

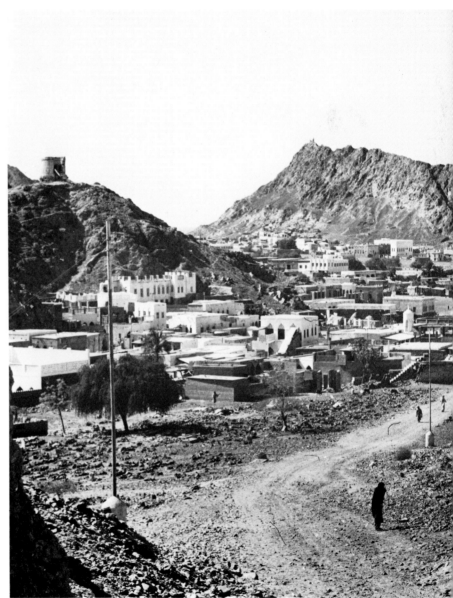

Right *Looking across Muscat from the pass to*
Sidab. 1967
  Far right *The government of India sent Sultan*
Faisal an unwanted present of useless cannons so
he made them into a barrier around Bait Graiza.

Below *The Ali Musa Mosque, Muscat.*

Right *The Sultan's palace, Bait al-Alam, at Muscat. The wing on the right, known as the Bait al-Barza, was the Minister of Interior's office and the gathering place for notables on 'Id days. 1969*

Below *A corridor of Bait al-Barza. 1968*

Below *The British Bank of the Middle East, centre, was the first modern building outside the walls of Muscat. 1951*

Above, right *The entrance to the British Consulate. 1951*

Right *Riyam, between Muscat and Muttrah, 1951. The bay was filled in when the new corniche road was built.*

Below *Muttrah Fort. 1965*
Right *Sidab from the pass. 1967*

Right *The beach at Sidab. 1967*

Left *Muttrah from the air. 1966*
    Below *The Luwatiyah quarter of Muttrah.*
1968

Below *The Ruwi gate, an internal customs post and traffic checkpoint, between Bait al-Falaj and Ras al-Hamra. 1964*

Right *Mina al-Fahal, the industrial area of the oil company, then called Saih al-Malih. 1966*

Below *The hot spring at Bosher at the base of the mountains. 1950*

Right *The Qadhi of Bosher and the Wali of Bosher. 1928*

The Wali of Muttrah goes for his first drive. 1928

The fort at Bait al-Falaj was for many years the military headquarters. 1928

Far left *Donkey boys at Ghala. 1928*

Left *House of a prosperous cultivator at Seeb. Houses made of palm fronds were cool and comfortable. 1928*

Below, left *Furnace for cooking dates in Seeb oasis, 1928. The four pillars are designed to support a roof over the cooking pots. The chimney is on the left.*

Above, right *The* shasha, *a fishing boat made of palm stems. 1929*

Below, right *The Murphys' car at Wataiyah, not far from Muttrah, on its first trip in Oman. 1928*

Overleaf *Camel train at Ruwais, on the way to the Interior, on the Company road. 1966*